FLORA'S GEMS
The
Little Book of

TULIPS

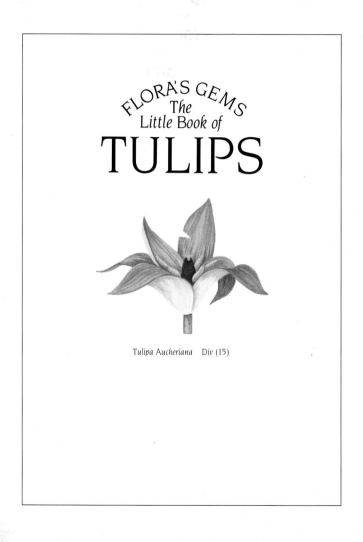

Tulipa Aucheriana   Div (15)

PRINSES IRENE
SINGLE EARLY Div (1)

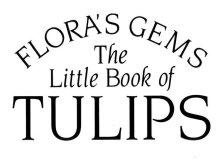

FLORA'S GEMS
The
Little Book of
TULIPS

by PAMELA TODD
Illustrated by IAN PENNEY

A Garden of
Poetry, History, Lore & Floriculture

A Bulfinch Press Book
LITTLE, BROWN AND COMPANY
Boston · New York · Toronto · London

First Edition

ISBN 0-8212-2101-9

Library of Congress Catalog Card Number 93-86017

A CIP catalogue record for this book is available from the British
Library

Conceived, edited and designed by David Fordham.

Published simultaneously in the United States of America by
Bulfinch Press, an imprint and trademark of Little, Brown and
Company (Inc.), in Great Britain by Little, Brown and Company (UK)
Ltd, and in Canada by Little, Brown & Company (Canada) Limited

PRINTED AND BOUND IN ITALY

ACKNOWLEDGEMENTS

The poem 'Tulip' is reproduced by permission of Curtis Brown London on
behalf of the Estate of Vita Sackville-West.

The author wishes to thank Wendy Akers of the Wakefield and North of
England Tulip Society and the librarians at the Royal Horticultural Society's
Lindley Library for their expert help and advice.

The author has used her best endeavours to clear all copyright material and
apologises in advance to any elusive authors.

CONTENTS

Above: PINK BEAUTY   *Div* (1)

ORANJE NASSAU
DOUBLE EARLY   Div (2)

INTRODUCTION

Yet rich as morn of many hue
When flashing clouds through darkness strike,
The tulip's petals shine in dew
All beautiful, yet none alike.

JAMES MONTGOMERY (1771-1854)

CARMINE-SCARLET STREAKED WITH INDIAN yellow, deep rose flushed with white; plum, golden yellow, or fragile pinks luminous with loveliness; fringed, feathered, splashed with every imaginable colour and colour combination, tulips are enchanting flowers – versatile, beautiful and brimful of spring. Their clean lines and sleek shape have made them a favourite decorative motif on porcelain and glass, in needlework, furniture and textiles, glazed tiles and even wrought-iron railings.

For centuries they have inspired writers, poets and painters, including Breughel, Cézanne, Dufy, Matisse and more recently David Hockney and Elizabeth Blackadder. The tulip symbolizes love, which is perhaps why Rubens chose to paint his second wife, Helen Fourment, in her tulip garden. Robert Herrick compared his mistress to one; Andrew Marvell lamented man's perverse desire to tinker with so natural a beauty; Elizabeth Barrett Browning asso-

MARÉCHAL NIEL
Div (2)

ciated tulips with children and Vita Sackville-West saw something bold and military in the tulip's erect bearing. Alexandre Dumas Père devoted a whole novel – La Tulipe Noire – to a fabled black one.

Surprisingly, Shakespeare makes no mention of tulips, although they had been introduced to England from the East during his lifetime and a number of varieties were grown in the garden of his near neighbour, the Elizabethan herbalist, John Gerard. However, Gerard admits that they were 'strange and forreine' flowers and describes seven sorts in his Herball (1597), including an early flowering red and a late flowering yellow. There is also one which sounds as if it had the beginnings of 'breaking', that is, where the tulip's solid colour splits up into stripes and becomes 'feathered' or 'flamed' with another colour. The flowers were known as florists' tulips in the seventeenth century, and are now classified as Rembrandt tulips.

I am a flow'r for sight, a drug for use,
By secret virtue and resistless power
Those whom the jaundice seizes I restore;
The dropsie headlong makes away
As soon as I my arms display.

ABRAHAM COWLEY (1616-67)

The tulip has long been thought to hold medicinal properties. The first-century Greek herbalist Dioscorides attributed aphrodisiac powers to the seed although John Parkinson, who made some scientific experiments of his own in 1629, confesses, 'for force of Venereous quality, I cannot say, either from myself, not having eaten many, or from any other on whome I had bestowed them'. Parkinson found the tulip more 'profitable for them that have a convulsion in their necke (which wee call a cricke in the necke) if it be drunke in harsh (that is, red) wine'.

Both Parkinson and John Gerard recommended the roots preserved in sugar as 'a good and wholesome sweet with tonic properties'. And Parkinson states, 'That the roots of tulips are nourishing there is no doubt, for divers have had them sent by their friends from beyond seas and mistaking them to be onions have used them in their pottage or broth'. More recently, the French writer Colette also records how in time of famine tulip bulbs were boiled and eaten.

ROMANTIC FABLES AND EXOTIC ORIGINS

> As then the Tulip from her morning sup
> Of Heav'nly vintage from the soil looks up,
> Do you devoutly do the like, till Heav'n
> To Earth invert you – like an empty Cup.
>
> RUBÁIYÁT OF OMAR KHAYYÁM (c.1015-1123)

THE TULIP HAS A LONG AND ROMANTIC PAST. Thousands of years ago it flourished wild across a wide area stretching from the eastern coast of the Mediterranean to the farthest reaches of China. It features in Christian and Islamic art and its tidy turban shape has been found on an illuminated bible dating from the twelfth century, and depicted surrounding the Madonna and Child on a fifteenth-century mural in Coventry Cathedral, though it was sadly reduced to rubble during the Second World War. Tulips also decorate the border of a miniature painting of the Mogul Emperor Shah Jahan (1628-58), the ardent husband who built the Taj Mahal as a mausoleum for his favourite wife, Mumtaz Mahal.

There is a Persian fable, related by the fourteenth-century poet, Hafiz, which celebrates the amorous associations of the tulip. A young, hopelessly in love couple, Ferhad and Shirin, discovered that the path of true love never

GARDEN PARTY
TRIUMPH   Div (3)

KANSAS   *Div* (3)

did run smooth when Ferhad was sent by the jealous king to a distant site to oversee a piece of elaborate statuary so vast and intricate that most thought it impossible to complete in the lifetime of any man. The site was a distant one but Ferhad set to work with a will. When, after some years, the king was informed by his spies that the project was nearing completion and was a wonderful piece of work, he panicked and sent a messenger to Ferhad informing him that Shirin had died. Demented with grief (and no doubt overwork), the frenzied lover leapt on his horse and rode straight off the edge of a rocky escarpment. Where the ground was splashed with his blood a red flower resembling his turban was said to have sprung up.

So the red tulip came to signify consuming love as Sir John Chardin, an Anglo-French jeweller travelling in Persia in the 1660s, reported in a letter home to his friends: 'When a young man presents one to his mistress, he gives her to

GUDOSHNIK   *Div* (4)

understand, by the general colour of the flower, that he is
on fire with her beauty: and by the black base of it, that his
heart is burnt to a coal.' The Victorians enlarged the vocab-
ulary of the tulip during their passion for the language of
flowers and created separate meanings for individual
colours, thus the yellow tulip signified 'hopeless love', the
purple 'undying love' and a streaked one spoke of 'beautiful eyes'. The Victorian volume *Birthday Gems*, published
in 1836, designates the purple tulip as the birthday flower
for those born on 21 March and the yellow for those born
on 17 May.

> *And where the tulip, following close behind*
> *The feet of Spring, her scarlet chalice rears,*
> *There Ferhad for the love of Shirin pined,*
> *Dyeing the desert red with his heart's tears.*
>
> Hafiz (c.1390)

ELIZABETH ARDEN
DARWIN HYBRID   *Div* (4)

GIFT OF THE FAIRIES

There's fairy tulips in the east,
The gardens of the sun;
The very streams reflect the hues,
And blossom as they run.

THE TULIP IS SUPPOSED TO BE ONE OF THE flowers loved by fairies and elves, who protected those who cultivated them. An old Hindustani story, *Rose of Bakawali*, describes the beautiful fairy of heaven who caused the tulips to 'immerse itself in blood because of the jealousy it entertained of her charming lips'.

From Devon there is an old folk tale that tells of fairies putting their babies to sleep at night in the satiny cups of tulips. They were so grateful to the old woman who owned the garden that they arranged for the tulips to take on bright colours and to smell as sweet as the rose – although they revoked the fragrance after their patroness died and was replaced by a hard, money-making man who destroyed the flower garden and replanted it with a parsley patch. In revenge the fairies tore up the parsley and danced on its leaves which is said to be why they grow so ragged.

THE FLOWER OF SULTANS AND SERAGLIOS

And, such being used in Eastern bowers,
Young maids may wonder if the flowers
Or meanings be the sweeter.

FROM 'A FLOWER IN A LETTER'
BY ELIZABETH BARRETT BROWNING (1806-61)

T HE TULIP WAS SO CELEBRATED IN TURKEY THAT it became the court flower during the reign of Sultan Suleiman I (1494-1566). It was already an elegant, carefully cultivated flower, although in looks quite unlike the garden tulip we cherish today. Then it was most prized for a tight, almond-shaped cup with arching, dagger-shaped petals which radiated out at the top into six sharp points, like a star.

It was an extravagant period of Turkish history, dominated by an extravagant ruler. Suleiman I was a poet of some repute, a philosopher and a great lover of flowers who filled his gardens with tulips of every colour. He was also a formidable military strategist with a vast empire, which, by 1532, had spread to within a few miles of Vienna. A corridor of trade was opened and, to the diplomats, travellers and merchants who visited Constantinople in the sixteenth century, it was the most beautiful city in the

PANDION   *Div* (5)

world. The harmony of the architecture and the grace and opulence of the Sultans' private gardens, filled with vast quantities of an exciting new flower, impressed them deeply. Each year, during a full moon, homage would be paid to this flamboyant flower with a Feast of Tulips. The seraglio (harem) gardens would be decorated with oriental magnificence and brilliantly illuminated to show the tulips off to their best advantage. One report tells of tortoises with candles on their backs being released in the evening to roam among the tulip beds.

Suleiman's son by the Russian slave, Roxelana, Sultan Selim II, started the first great wave of 'tulipomania', sending orders to remote parts of Turkey for as many as fifty thousand bulbs at one time 'for my royal gardens'. It is probably he who was responsible for the extinction of the parent species in the wild. But the Turkish love affair with the tulip reached its height during the reign of Ahmed III

(1703-30), a period historically known as the *Lalé Devri*, or Tulip Period. This was when Turkey became the floricultural centre of the world and it was forbidden to buy or sell tulips outside the capital on pain of exile, causing a French tulip merchant named Fachat to remark that in Turkey a tulip bulb was more highly valued than a human life. At the Turkish court the tulip festivals became even more extravagant, as shown by this description of one in a letter from the French Ambassador, writing in April 1726, to Louis XV:

When the tulips are in flower, and the Grand Vizier (Ibrahim Pasha) wishes to show them to the Sultan, care is taken to fill the gaps where the tulips have come up blind, by flowers taken from other gardens and placed in bottles. Beside every fourth flower is stood a candle, level with the bloom, and along the alleys are hung cages filled with all kinds of birds. The trellises are all decorated with an enormous quantity of flowers of every sort, placed in bottles and lit by an infinite number of glass lamps of different colours. These lamps are also hung on the green branches of shrubs which are specially transplanted for the fête from neighbouring woods and placed behind the trellises. The effect of all these varied colours, and of the lights which are reflected by countless mirrors, is magnificent. The illuminations, and the noisy consort of Turkish musical instruments which accompanies them, continue nightly so long as the tulips remain in flower, during which time the Grand Seigneur and his whole suite are lodged and fed at the expense of the Grand Vizier.

LA TULIPE NOIRE
SINGLE LATE   Div (5)

FROM CONSTANTINOPLE TO THE WEST

The gardens fire with a joyful blaze
Of Tulips in the morning's rays.
RALPH WALDO EMERSON (1803-82)

MODERN TRAVEL AND COMMUNICATIONS HAVE become so efficient that it is difficult to imagine the excitement felt over four hundred years ago on discovering a new species of flower and the dangers, adventures and rewards involved in bringing it home. The sixteenth century was a time of expanding horizons, both geographic and scientific, and of colourful, resourceful characters. We owe the arrival of the tulip in the West to one of these men. He was Ogier Ghislain de Busbecq (1522-92), a Flemish diplomat and the Ambassador of the Emperor Ferdinand I to the court of Suleiman the Magnificent. He was an educated man and curious about the world. In 1554 he wrote enthusiastically to his friends about a new flower he saw growing between Adrianople and Constantinople, although he misunderstood his guide and took the description of the flower as 'turban-shaped'—*tülband*—for its name. In fact, in Central Asia, tulips were always called *lalé*.

SEED PODS

As we passed we saw everywhere abundance of flowers, such as the Narcissus, Hyacinths, and those called by the Turks Tulipam, not without great astonishment on account of the time of the year, as it was then the middle of winter, a season so unfriendly to flowers. ... The Tulipam have little or no smell but are admired for their beauty and variety of colour. The Turks pay great attention to the cultivation of flowers, nor do they hesitate, though by no means extravagant, to expend several aspers for one that is beautiful. I received several presents of these flowers, which cost me not a little.

Busbecq wasted no time in sending some seed to his great friend Carolus Clusius, a Flemish doctor also known as Charles de L'Ecluse, who lived from 1526-1609, and who was then Prefect of the Royal Medicinal Garden in Prague. Clusius was a dedicated man of science as well as a keen practical gardener and he applied himself assiduously to the

MAGIER
SINGLE LATE   Div (5)

cultivation of tulips. He had great success. Busbecq kept him supplied with seed – Clusius mentions having obtained yellow, red, white and purple self-coloured flowers, as well as 'broken' forms from a batch received in 1573. Matteo Caccini (c.1573-1640), a Florentine botanist and dealer in rare plants, also sent him bulbs. By the time Clusius left Prague to take up his post as Prefect of the Botanical Gardens in Leiden in 1592 he had over six hundred bulbs. Clusius however was jealous of his new flower and would not share the bulbs with anyone. Some reports suggest that he offered them at scandalously high prices, others that he refused to sell them at all. The result was that one winter many of his bulbs were stolen and Clusius, discouraged by the whole affair, gave up his work with tulips and never grew them again.

Others did, though, and the flower's popularity spread through Europe with surprising speed. Conrad Gesner, the Swiss horticulturalist who attempted to reclassify plants according to the shape of their leaves and who came to be known as the German Pliny, was the first to record seeing a tulip flowering in Western Europe in the garden of 'the ingenious and learned Councillor Herwart'. In his *De Hortis Germaniae*, he describes it as: 'growing with one large reddish flower, like a red lily, having eight petals of which four are outside, and just as many within, with a pleasant smell, soothing and delicate, which soon leaves it.'

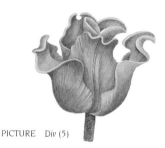

PICTURE *Div* (5)

Tulipa gesneriana was the collective name given to the tulips introduced to Europe from Turkey from 1554 onwards. These are thought to be the parents of all our garden tulips and, as such, are immensely important.

In 1562 a cargo of bulbs from Constantinople arrived in Antwerp, but they were sufficiently strange then to baffle the good burghers who, the story goes, first tried eating them, but on finding them unpleasant, threw the rest onto a midden where they eventually flowered. (For a short period enterprising gastronomers did try to make a delicacy out of tulip bulbs and they were eaten in Germany with sugar, and in England spiced with oil and vinegar, but the fashion was a fleeting one.)

Exactly when tulips arrived in England is not known, but they were certainly grown before the end of the sixteenth century. We find practical advice on cultivating them in Thomas Hill's *The Gardener's Labyrinth* (1577) and Richard

MARJOLEIN   *Div* (6)

Hakluyt in his *Brief Remembrance of Things to be Endeavoured at Constantinople* (1582) mentions that 'within these foure yeeres there have been brought into England from Vienna in Austria divers kinds of flowers called Tulipas, and these and others procured thither a little before them from Constantinople by an excellent man called M. Carolus Clusius.'

John Gerard, the industrious and influential herbalist, whose garden at Holborn contained over a thousand plants – 'all manner of strange trees, herbes, rootes, plants and flowers' – grew tulips and had an energetic friend, James Garret, 'a curious searcher of Simples, and learned Apothecarie in London', who had been experimenting for twenty years with different kinds of tulips 'all of which to describe particularlie, were to roule Sisiphus stone, or number the sandes', which gives some idea of the abundance of tulip cultivars available in England at the end of the sixteenth century.

Tulips

Let tulips trust not the warm vernal rain,
But dread the frosts and still their blooms restrain;
So when bright Phoebus smiles with kindly care,
The moon not sullied by a lowering air,
Early the beauteous race you'll wondering see,
Ranged in the beds, a numerous progeny:
The tulip with her painted charm display
Through the mild air, and make the garden gay;
The tulip which with gaudy colours stained,
The name of beauty to her race has gained,
For whether she in scarlet does delight,
Chequered and streaked with lines of glittering white,
Or sprinkled o'er with purple charms our sight;
Or widow-like beneath a sable veil,
Her purest lawn does artfully conceal,
Or emulate, the varied agate's veins,
From every flower the beauty's prize obtained.

ABRAHAM COWLEY (1618-67)

The tulip was late reaching France. There is no record of a bulb flowering until 1608, but soon after this and especially during the reign of the sun king, Louis XIV, no lady of fashion would be seen in the spring without a rare bloom adorning her dress, particularly since they were becoming spectacularly expensive.

WEST POINT
LILY-FLOWERED   Div (6)

BELLFLOWER
FRINGED   Div (7)

For a single bulb of the rare 'Mère Brune' a miller exchanged his mill; a young Frenchman was offered just one bulb of a rare tulip appropriately christened 'Mariage de ma fille' by his father-in-law as his daughter's dowry. Yet another fanatic swapped his brewery, valued at thirty thousand francs, for a bulb afterwards known as 'Tulipe brasserie'. The craze for tulips was spreading northwards to Holland where it was to explode into a passion of dangerous proportions. In England, where aristocratic patrons were conceiving and executing some of the great formal gardens, the fame of the tulip was threatening to eclipse that of the rose and the daffodil.

THE TULIP

There is lately a flower (shall I call it so? in courtesie I will tearme it so, though it deserve not the appellation) a Toolip, which hath engrafted the love and affections of most people unto it; and what is this Toolip? A well complexion'd stink, an ill favour wrapt up in pleasant colours; as for the use thereof in physick, no physitian hath honoured it yet with the mention, nor with a Greek, or Latin name, so inconsiderable hath it hitherto been accompted; and yet this is that which filleth all gardens, hundreds of pounds being given for the root thereof, whilst I the Rose, am neglected and contemned and conceived beneath the honour of noble hands, and fit only to grow in the gardens of yeomen.

ANTHEOLOGIA OF THE SPEECH OF FLOWERS
BY THOMAS FULLER (1608-61)

In 1611 the Earl of Salisbury sent John Tradescant the Elder to the Continent to buy plants for the great mansion – Hatfield House – he was building in the country. Tradescant (c.1570-1638) was an early, pioneering example of that now familiar and important figure in English gardening – the knowledgeable plantsman. In Haarlem that year he purchased eight hundred tulip bulbs at ten shillings per hundred, but was soon back buying bulbs by the ton.

Many beautiful engravings of tulips were included in Crispin van der Pass's exquisite *Hortus Floridus* (1614), but it was John Parkinson, one of the great fathers of English gardening, who first did full justice to the flower. In his *Paradisi in Sole: Paradisus Terrestris* or 'A Garden of Pleasant Flowers' (1629) he includes a hundred and forty varieties, 'all now made denizens in our Gardens, where they yield us more delight and more encrease for their proportion than they did unto their owne naturals'. The engravings may have been lovelier in Crispin van der Pass's book, but Parkinson was more practical, including extensive descriptions of the flower he called 'the Turkes cap' and advice on cultivation from the sowing of seeds to bringing them to flower, and advice on 'drying off' the older established plant. He describes flower lovers as being 'more delighted in the search, curiosity and rarities of these pleasant delights than any age I think before' and talks of 'the admirable varieties of colours that daily doe arise in them . . . that the

ARTIST
VIRIDIFLORA   Div (8)

HUMMINGBIRD   *Div* (8)

place where they stand may resemble a piece of curious needlework or a piece of painting. . . . Besides this glory of variety in colours that these flowers have, they carry so stately and delightfull a forme, and do abide so long in their bravery (enduring three whole months from the first unto the last) that there is no Lady or Gentlewoman of any worth that is not caught with this delight or not delighted with these flowers.'

John Tradescant was a great tulip fancier. He grew fifty varieties in his garden at Lambeth and when he was appointed gardener to King Charles I and his French-born queen Henrietta Maria in 1630, tulips rapidly became great favourites at court.

During the troubled Civil War years many Royalists chose to retire to their country estates and keep a low pro-file. One such was Sir Thomas Hanmer (1612-78), who was married to one of Queen Henrietta Maria's maids of

REMBRANDTS
Div (9)

honour. Sir Thomas was a great tulip enthusiast and cultivated them in a large flowerbed in full view of his country
house at Bettisfield in Shropshire where he could see 'The
Queene of Bulbous plants whose flower is so beautiful in
its figure and more rich and admirable in colours and wonderful variety of markings'.

Sir Thomas was generous with his bulbs, making presents of them to friends. He left notes on their culture:

Set them in the ground about the full moon in September about
four inches asunder and under four inches deep, set the early
ones where the sun in the spring may come hot on them. Set the
later kinds where the noon sun may not be too fierce on them.
Let the earth be mould taken from the fields, or where wood-
stacks have been, and mix it with a fourth part or more of sand.
Make your beds at least half a yard thick of this mould. Tulips live
best planted alone, but you may put some anemones with them
on the outside of the beds if they be raised high and round.

WEBER'S PARROT
PARROT   Div (10)

The nurseryman John Rea (author of *Flora, Ceres and Pomona* (1665)) was a neighbour of Sir Thomas in Shropshire. Rea was one of the great tulip enthusiasts working at a time when tulips were, of course, reaching cult status in Holland. He used his summer house not merely 'for delight and entertainment', but also as an excellent place for drying his tulip bulbs. He also devised a series of portable canvas tilts to protect his tulips from the wind, hot sun or showers which might be 'prejudicial to their different yet admirable complexions'.

Samuel Gilbert, who was married to Rea's daughter Minerva, said Rea 'had the largest collection of Tulips of any man in England' and described his father-in-law as 'the best florist of his time'. He was reputed to have more than two hundred varieties which he divided into 'earlies', 'mid-seasons' and 'lates'. His collection included the famous 'Semper Augustus' which played such an important part in the Dutch drama. Gilbert continued Rea's work and in his own book, *Florists Vade Mecum* (1683), he gives a plan of a garden for tulips, in which the beds are divided into fifty squares, each intended for a distinct variety.

Tulips arrived in America in the luggage and among the personal possessions of the early settlers, many of whom were Dutch, and became a common motif in paintings and decorations of domestic objects like quilts and dishes. In 1655 Adrian van der Donck wrote that the Hollanders were

BLUE PARROT
Div (10)

growing fine tulips in New Amsterdam and New Nether-
lands (now New York), and according to a report made to
William Penn by Gabriel Thomas, John Tateham's 'Great
and Stately Palace' in Pennsylvania had tulips in its garden
in 1698.

Half a century later a list of seeds available from a local
nursery printed in a Boston newspaper dated 30 March
1760 included '50 Different Sorts of Mixed Tulip Roots'.

The statesman Thomas Jefferson (1743-1826), who had
visited some of the new landscape gardens in Europe
during the 1780s, created his own beautiful garden at Mon-
ticello, Western Virginia, where tulips 'like belles of the
day' had a special place.

For Jefferson, gardening was a continual delight. In 1811
he wrote that 'No occupation is so delightful to me as the
culture of the earth. . . . But though an old man, I am but a
young gardener.'

Tulipomania in Holland

The tulip white did for complexion seek,
And learned to interline its cheek;
Its onion root they then so high did hold,
That one was for a meadow sold.

'The Mower Against Gardens' by
Andrew Marvell (1621-78)

T HE TULIP FANCIER IN MARVELL'S POEM MAY HAVE secured himself a bargain, paying just the one meadow for a single tulip bulb. At the height of tulipomania, which raged unchecked across Holland in the seventeenth century and reached its frenzied height between 1634 and 1637, bulbs were fetching fantastic sums. A single 'Viceroy' bulb was exchanged for '2 lasts of Wheat, 4 of Rye, 4 fat oxen, 3 fat swine, 12 fat sheep, 2 hogsheads of wine, 4 tuns of beer, 2 tons of butter, 1,000 pounds of cheese, a bed, a complete suit of clothes and a silver beaker – value of the whole, 2,500 florins'. But that too was cheap compared to the price of four thousand six hundred florins, plus a new carriage and pair, which was paid for a single bulb of the highly prized 'Semper Augustus'.

What caused all the excitement was the unpredictable tendency of the self-coloured tulips, later known as 'breeders', to 'break' and produce a new flower striped or splashed with colour. We now know this to be caused by a virus transmitted by aphis, but then it was an intriguing, though profitable, mystery. Growers experimented by plunging their bulbs into murky combinations of ashes and dye, or by starving them of nutrients.

Cornelius van Baerle, the tulip-obsessed hero of Alexandre Dumas' novel, *La Tulipe Noire*, succeeds, with the aid of the lovely Rosa, in growing the first black in an unlikely mixture while in jail. Here's his breathless first glimpse of the unique flower:

Cornelius, hardly daring to breathe, touched the tip of the flower with his lips; and never did kiss upon woman's lips, even though they were such lips as Rosa's, touch the heart so deeply.

The tulip was lovely, magnificent, superb; its stalk was more than eighteen inches high; it grew from the folds of four green leaves, slender and straight as lance-shafts; and the whole of the flower was as black and shining as jet.

Fortunes were being made and people from all walks of life became swept up in the gamble. 'Often did a nobleman purchase of a chimney-sweep Tulips to the amount of 2,000 florins, and sell them at the same time to a farmer, and neither the nobleman, chimney-sweep nor farmer had roots in their possession nor wished to possess them'.

Despite public notices 'Warning all good Citizens of our beloved country against the threat of those who call them-

ANGÉLIQUE
DOUBLE LATE   Div (11)

EROS *Div* (11)

selves Florists', the trade continued covertly in taverns in every town. And, at first, everyone appeared to win. Workmen sold their tools to buy bulbs and stood to gain, in a few months, houses, coaches and horses. Colossal sums were pledged during the three years the mania raged.

Of course it was all folly on a grand scale. The speculators were gambling on something as elusive as the wind and in time it did come to be called the windtrade. It was a madness, a highly contagious but profitable fever. Those caught up in it were ridiculed in print and reviled from pulpits by preachers who tried urgently to stem 'this moral decline'. A satirical painting entitled 'Flora's Wagon of Idiots' by Henrik Gerritszoon Pot (1585-1637) shows a large, wheeled sailing craft in which Flora sits holding a cornucopia filled with tulips in one hand and in the other three individual blooms labelled 'Semper Augustus', 'General Bol' and 'Admiral van Hoorn'. Keeping her company are three florists named

'Good-for-nothing', 'Eager rich' and 'Tippler', who sport ludicrous head gear out of which tulips grow like cuckolds' horns. In the front of the ship sit two sinister, two-faced women called 'Idle Hope' and 'Miser', who stretch forlornly after the Bird of Hope. The vessel travels over ground strewn with tulips and is followed by a crowd of rustics trampling their tools in their eagerness, shouting 'We will sail with you too'. In the distance a similar craft can be seen wrecked and broken.

The warnings, however, went unheeded and in the spring of 1637 the crash came. The amateurs who had jumped on the bandwagon were impatient for wealth and suddenly everyone was selling and no one wanted to buy. Bulbs which just a few weeks before had changed hands (figuratively, of course, for the bulbs were generally in the ground) up to ten times a day, now excited no interest. The bubble had burst. Thousands were ruined and the Estates General, or Parliament, was forced to step in to annul all speculative agreements made that year. They set a maximum value for a tulip bulb of fifty florins. 'Semper Augustus' was now worth one-hundredth of its former value. Many were bankrupted, lives were ruined and it took years for Holland's economy to recover from the blow the madness had dealt it, but the people of Holland kept faith with the tulip and it is now one of the steadiest commercial cornerstones in the country's economy.

THE FIRST
KAUFMANNIANA   *Div* (12)

TULIP SOCIETIES & BLOOMING BUSINESS

The gay gaudy tulip observe as you walk,
How flaunting the gloss of its vest!
How proud! and how stately it stands on its stalk,
In beauty's diversity drest!

FROM 'SERENE IS THE MORNING'
BY WILLIAM WOTY (1731-91)

THE ENGLISH, WHILE UNDOUBTEDLY CHARMED BY tulips, proved immune to the frenzy of tulipomania. When tulips were offered as a commodity on the London Stock Exchange the year before the Dutch crash came in 1637, they flopped dismally. However, on the Continent they continued to be prized by the rich and powerful. They were popular in all European courts, but perversely it was their very popularity that caused them to lose favour with the English aristocracy.

It was left to the working man to cultivate the 'perfect' tulip – a standard for which had been set down by Philip Miller in his *Gardener's Dictionary* (1731). Tom Storer, a railroad engineer from Derby, grew his tulips alongside the railroad track and became a highly regarded tulip expert; William Clark of Croydon created the famous 'Polyphemus' from one of his seedling 'breeder' tulips and is regarded by some as the father of the English florists' tulip.

BERLIOZ   D*iv* (12)

For some tulips were an obsession. The H*orticultural Magazine* of June 1847 records that a Dulwich florist was so attached to his tulips that one frosty night he covered them with blankets taken from his bed, caught cold and died.

Tulip societies, like the Wakefield and North of England Society which still thrives today, were formed and tulips were shown up and down the country. An 'Account of the Different Flower Shows held in Lancashire, Cheshire, York-shire, etc. for the year 1820' gives a list of sixteen tulip shows held in the upstairs rooms of public houses. The Wakefield Society's two annual shows – one for Dutch and the other for English florists's tulips – are no longer held in public houses although the flowers are still exhibited in rich brown beer bottles.

In 1849 the National Tulip Society was formed to regulate standards and at the beginning of the twentieth century the collectively named cottage tulips were reclassified and

ROSANNA   *Div* (14)

divided into three separate categories: Darwin, English and Dutch tulips. It was enthusiasm for the tall, sturdy Darwins, whose stout stems enabled them to stand up to the rough winds and hail of an English May, that led to the setting up of an English bulb industry, in Spalding in Lincolnshire towards the end of the nineteenth century. Fenland similar to the silty soil of Holland was drained and converted to growing fields by Dutch bulb sellers who had settled in England, and by the 1920s flower production was in full force.

Tulips are now cultivated in other parts of Great Britain and indeed in other parts of the world – including Japan and the United States of America – but we still tend to associate tulips with Holland, where, despite the vicissitudes of tulipomania, Napoleon's occupation and the devastation of two world wars, the tulip industry continues to bloom. Every year tourists make the pilgrimage to the relatively small 'corridor' between Haarlem and Leiden, which is known as 'de Bollenstreek' (the bulb-growing region) where the trade is centred.

For a few weeks in the year the tulip fields detonate into the most brilliant colours, but their moment of glory is brief for as soon as the grower, whose interest lies in the bulb not the blossom, has established that the tulips are the colour, shape and type he wants, the flowers are all decapitated to allow the nourishment to return to the bulb. So Keukenhof Park was created in 1949 to provide an outdoor exhibition of many types of tulips blooming in all their splendour.

Spalding, too, have a twenty-five acre park, named Springfields, devoted to tulips. It also hosts a vast tulip festival. Similar festivals are held in many American towns in May, especially those that have a large population with Dutch ancestry, like Holland in Michigan, Pella and Orange City in Iowa, and Albany, New York.

Canada is home to hosts of tulips which came originally from Holland, an annual gift from the Dutch people to express their gratitude for the help of the Canadian Armed Forces in the liberation of their country during the Second World War and for the refuge given to Queen Juliana. An annual spring festival has been held in Ottawa since 1951 and has grown into the largest public display of tulips in North America. Tulip displays are also held in Vancouver, Montreal and Toronto.

JUAN

FOSTERIANA   *Div* (13)

TULIPS IN THE GARDEN

The tulip is the peacock among flowers:
the one has no scent, the other no song;
the one glories in its gown, the other in
its train.

FROM AN OLD FRENCH GARDENING BOOK

T ULIPS ARE VERY SIMPLE TO GROW AND WILL succeed in any reasonable garden soil which does not become waterlogged. There is really only one rule and that is to plant before the first frost. October and November are the best months. Buy good-sized bulbs and plant them to a depth of six inches, measuring from the bottom of the bulb to the surface of the soil. Place a small handful of sand at the bottom of the hole for extra drainage before putting in the bulb, flat side down. Large tulips should be planted five to eight inches apart in a sunny position. After they have flowered the leaves must be allowed to remain on the plant. This is the stage at which food is produced for next year's bulb, so snap off the dead flower to prevent it forming a seed pod, but leave the foliage until it has died down naturally. Then lift the bulbs and store them in a frost-free, airy place until the late autumn. With proper care the bulbs will improve and multiply.

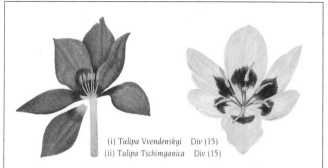

(i) *Tulipa Vvendenskyi*   Div (15)
(ii) *Tulipa Tschimganica*   Div (15)

The versatility and variety of tulips is astonishing, and what to plant and in which combinations is really down to the individual. Canon Henry Ellacombe (1822-1916) was a parson-gardener who wrote entertainingly for the *Guardian* during the years 1890 to 1893. He lived at the Vicarage in Bitton, near Bristol, for the whole of his life, which spanned the reign of Queen Victoria. He loved tulips although he had decided preferences. 'I am not very fond of the florists' tulip,' he wrote in his book *In a Gloucestershire Garden* (1895):

. . . in some cases their colours are most brilliant, but always coarse and flaring, and their growth very stiff, and to me they give little pleasure. Indeed, I think a bed consisting of tulips only is an ugly object; I should say that such a bed is the ugliest of all such one-flowered beds, except a bed of double-zinnias; but in so saying I suppose I am in a minority, and perhaps a very small minority.

ORATORIO
GREIGII   *Div* (14)

Here is a list of a few good companion plants with blossoms whose colours blend and harmonize with tulips to prevent this gardening gaffe: arabis, candytuft, English daisy, forget-me-not (especially effective with vivid pink tulips which appear from a distance to float above a sea of electric blue), lobelia, pansies, primroses, violas and wallflowers. The mid-season tulips combine well with other flowering bulbs such as hyacinths, crocuses and muscari, the lovely blue grape hyacinths. For those with the space and the inclination there are enough different colours and varieties of tulips to keep a garden iridescent with colour for almost three months.

Gertrude Jekyll, the great gardening legend, who, together with William Robinson, was responsible for the violent swing away from the regimented rows of bedding plants so beloved of the mid-Victorians, to the creative freedom of the herbaceous border, suggested using *Stachys lanata* (Lamb's ears) as an underplanting for tulips to mask the dying foliage. 'The first small grey spires shooting up in spring, interlaced with milk-white tulips produce an almost ethereal effect,' she writes in *Colour Schemes for the Flower Garden* (1908). She was famous for approaching the garden as a canvas and her 'drifts of colour' have been compared to Monet's garden paintings. In vast spring borders she describes mixing pale flowers such as primroses, daffodils, iris, wallflowers and anemones with long drifts of tulips.

Tulips are the great garden flowers in the last week of April and earliest days of May. . . . One of the best for graceful and delicate beauty is *tulipa retroflexa*, of a soft lemon-yellow colour, and twisted and curled petals; then 'Silver Crown', a white flower with a delicate picotee-like thread of scarlet along the edge of the sharply pointed and reflexed petals. A variety of this called 'Sulphur Crown' is only a little less beautiful. Then there is 'Golden Crown', also with pointed petals and occasional threadings of scarlet. Nothing is more gorgeous than the noble *Gesneriana major*, with its great chalice of crimson-scarlet and pools of blue in the inner base of each petal. The gorgeously flamed parrot tulips are indispensable, and the large double 'Yellow Rose', and the early double white 'La Candeur'.

FROM 'THE MAKING OF A GARDEN' BY GERTRUDE JEKYLL (1843-1932)

Vita Sackville-West's love affair with tulips started in 1926 when she first saw wild tulips growing in Persia, 'the white ones that are so sweet-scented, and the yellow ones that have no scent at all, but are of a beautiful pure buttercup yellow, like a pointed goblet designed by some early draughtsman with a right instinct for line'.

Vita Sackville-West liked profusion: 'Cram, cram, cram every chink and cranny'. She wanted her garden at Sissinghurst to be a romantic tumble of flowers and she believed in 'exaggeration; big groups, big masses; I am sure that it is more effective to plant twelve tulips together than to split them into two groups of six'.

(i) *Tulipa fosteriana*   Div (13)
(ii) *Tulipa julia*   Div (15)

TULIP

The tulips that have pushed a pointed tusk
In steady inches, suddenly resolve
Upon their gesture, earliest the royal
Princes of Orange and of Austria,
Their Courtier the little Duc de Thol,
And, since the State must travel with the Church,
In plum, shot crimson, couleur, Cardinal.

But grander than these dwarf diminutives,
Comes the tall Darwin with the waxing May,
Can stem so slender bear such sovereign head
Nor stoop with weight of beauty? See her pride
Equals her beauty, never grew so straight
A spire of faith, nor flew so bright a flag
Lacquered by brush strokes of the painting sun.

VITA SACKVILLE-WEST (1892-1962)

TULIPA ACUMINATA
OTHER SPECIES   *Div* (15)

CLASSIFICATION OF *Tulipa*

GARDEN HYBRIDS

EARLIES

1 *Single early tulips*: flowering time mid-April. 9-16in tall. Many of the oldest tulips in cultivation fall into this class. Examples include 'Keizerskroon', a red with a broad yellow edge, in cultivation since 1750. Also included are more recent introductions like the salmon feathered, soft orange 'Prinses Irene'.

2 *Double early tulips*: flowering time mid-April. 9-16in tall. Many-petalled, long-lasting blooms on strong stems. Examples are the white 'Schoonord' and orange-red 'Oranje Nassau'.

MID-SEASON

3 *Triumph tulips*: flowering time late April to early May. 16-24in tall. Strong-stemmed, robust and vigorous. Examples include the rose-pink, cone-shaped 'Garden Party' and the deep purple 'Attila'.

4 *Darwin hybrids*: flowering time early to mid-May. 24-30in tall. Strong-stemmed, extremely robust and vigorous with large, square-based flowers. Examples include the creamy yellow 'Ivory Floradale' and the rose-pink 'Elizabeth Arden'.

LATES

5 *Single late tulips*: flowering time early May. 24-30in tall. A large class including the popular Darwin and cottage tulips, as well as the Dutch and English breeder tulips. Examples include the deep purple-black 'La Tulipe Noire' and the carmine-red 'Halcro'.

6 *Lily-flowered tulips*: flowering time end of April. 20-24in tall. Long elegant flowers whose petals are pointed and curled back. Examples include the intensely yellow 'West Point' and the faintly green-streaked 'White Triumphator'.

7 *Fringed tulips*: flowering time mid-May. 18-26in tall. Similar to parrot tulips but neater with just the tips of their petals serrated into a short, spiky fringe. Examples include the wine-red 'Burgundy Lace' and creamy rose-pink 'Bellflower'.

LATES (*continued*)

8 *Viridiflora tulips*: flowering time mid-May. 10-21in tall. Unusual tulips characterized by a band of green of varying length and breadth on the outside of each petal. Examples include the green-streaked, deep rose-pink 'Esperanto' and rose-apricot and green 'Artist'.

9 *Rembrandt tulips*: flowering time mid-May. 18-22in tall. The so-called broken tulips with petals flecked or striped with another colour. Examples include the yellow and red 'Absalon' and the violet and white 'Gloire de Holland'.

10 *Parrot tulips*: flowering time mid-May. 20-26in tall. Extravagant flowers with frilled petals. Examples include the yellow and scarlet 'Flaming parrot' and the cream pink and green 'Weber's Parrot'.

11 *Double late tulips*: flowering time late May. 16-24in tall. Sometimes called peony-flowered tulips. Large blooms often need support. Examples include the pure pink 'Angélique' and the snow-white 'Mount Tacoma'.

SPECIES

Kaufmanniana: flowering time early March. 6-10in tall. Often called 'the water-lily tulip' as the pointed petals open flat in the sun into star shapes from a flower that is cone-shaped when closed. Examples include the red and white 'The First' and tiny pink and white 'Heart's Delight'.

Fosteriana: flowering time mid-April. 12-18in tall. The largest and most brilliant of the Central Asiatic tulips, with enormous flowers which can reach a span of 10in when fully open. Examples include the orange yellow 'Juan' and the fiery oriental red 'Madam Lefeber'.

Greigii: flowering time May. 8-12in tall. Long-lasting flowers on short stems with mottled, striped or spotted leaves. Examples include the apricot-rose 'Oratorio' and the red-edged sulphur 'Plaisir'.

Other species: flowering time April. Includes the slender pink and white T. *clusiana* or 'Lady Tulip', the dramatic pillar box red T. *praestans* and the curious T. *acuminata* with its narrow tapering petals ending in an almost thread-like point.